A NOTE TO PARENTS

When your children are ready to "step into reading," giving them the right books—and lots of them—is as crucial as giving them the right food to eat. **Step into Reading Books** present exciting stories and information reinforced with lively, colorful illustrations that make learning to read fun, satisfying, and worthwhile. They are priced so that acquiring an entire library of them is affordable. And they are beginning readers with an important difference—they're written on four levels.

Step 1 Books, with their very large type and extremely simple vocabulary, have been created for the very youngest readers. **Step 2 Books** are both longer and slightly more difficult. **Step 3 Books,** written to mid-second-grade reading levels, are for the child who has acquired even greater reading skills. **Step 4 Books** offer exciting nonfiction for the increasingly proficient reader.

Children develop at different ages. **Step into Reading Books,** with their four levels of reading, are designed to help children become good—and interested—readers *faster*. The grade levels assigned to the four steps—preschool through grade 1 for Step 1, grades 1 through 3 for Step 2, grades 2 and 3 for Step 3, and grades 2 through 4 for Step 4—are intended only as guides. Some children move through all four steps very rapidly; others climb the steps over a period of several years. These books will help your child "step into reading" in style!

To Fran Penner

C.1 1996

Text copyright © 1995 by Lucille Recht Penner. Illustrations copyright © 1995 by Jada Rowland. All rights reserved under International and Pan-American Copyright Conventions. Published in the United States by Random House, Inc., New York, and simultaneously in Canada by Random House of Canada Limited, Toronto.

Library of Congress Cataloging-in-Publication Data:
Penner, Lucille Recht.
The Statue of Liberty / by Lucille Recht Penner ; illustrated by Jada Rowland.
p. cm. — (Step into reading. Step 1 book)
ISBN: 0-679-86928-X (trade) — 0-679-96928-4 (lib. bdg.)
1. Statue of Liberty (New York, N.Y.)—Juvenile literature. 2. New York (N.Y.)—Buildings, structures, etc.—Juvenile literature. I. Rowland, Jada, ill.
II. Title. III. Series. F128.64.L6P48 1995 974.7′1—dc20 95-1854

Manufactured in the United States of America   10 9 8 7 6 5 4 3 2 1

STEP INTO READING is a trademark of Random House, Inc.

Step into Reading™

The Statue of Liberty

by Lucille Recht Penner

illustrated by Jada Rowland

A Step 1 Book

Random House 🏠 New York

A lady stands in
New York Harbor.
She is as tall as a
skyscraper.
She is called
the Statue of Liberty.

"Liberty" means freedom.
All over the world,
people dreamed
of coming to America
to find freedom.

People came by ship.

The trip took many days.

Men, women, and children
were crowded together.

They were tired, hungry,
and scared.

Suddenly they saw the lady!
They had reached
America at last.
Now they knew
they were free.
People cried for joy.

The Statue of Liberty

was a present

from the people of France

to the people of the

United States.

A Frenchman made the lady.

His name was

Frédéric Bartholdi.

He copied his mother's face

for his statue.

How beautiful she was!

First Frédéric made
a small statue.

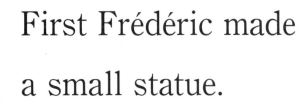

Then a bigger one.

Then an even
bigger one.

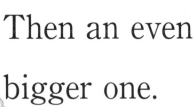

The last statue
was so big
it could not fit
in his workshop!

He had to make it

in pieces.

He made the right hand

holding the torch.

Then he made

the head.

Each finger was longer
than a man.
Each eye was as big
as a child.

Frédéric needed
lots of help.
His helpers worked
in a big room.

They took
the pieces outside
and put them together.
She was higher than
all the buildings.
Much higher!

19

Workers took
the statue apart.
They packed it
in 214 crates.

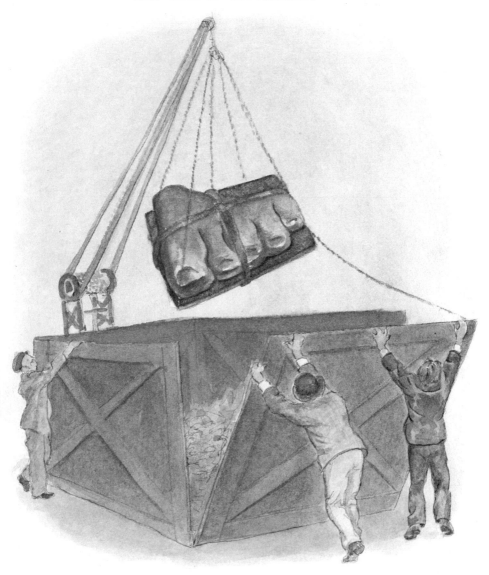

A ship carried it
from France to New York.

In America

the people

were building

a high pedestal

for the lady to stand on.

But they ran
out of money!
The work stopped.
No one knew
what to do.

Joseph Pulitzer owned

a newspaper.

He had an idea.

Joseph said, "The statue
needs a home!
I will print the name
of everyone who gives
money to help."
Thousands of people
sent nickels and dimes.
Children sent pennies.
Soon there was
enough money.

Now workers could finish
the huge pedestal.
They set the lady
on top of it.

A big French flag
was draped over her face.

On October 28, 1886,
the people of New York
had a parade
to welcome her.

The President of
the United States
made a speech.
Frédéric Bartholdi
was excited!
He raced up a staircase
inside the statue.
Up and up he went
to the very top.

Frédéric looked down.

A boy was waving

a white handkerchief.

It was the signal.

Frédéric pulled a rope

and the flag fell.

There was the lady!

Hip, hip, hurrah!

Cannons boomed.

Boat whistles blew.

People cheered.

The excitement
never ended.
Today, more than
one hundred years later,
the Statue of Liberty
still welcomes people
to America—
the land of the free.